Roofless

By Stuart Harvey and First Stop Darlington

Roofless

By Stuart Harvey and First Stop Darlington

ISBN: 9781912092659

First published in 2017 by Arkbound Ltd (Publishers)

Cover design by Laura Mochrie

Arkbound is a social enterprise that aims to promote social inclusion, community development and artistic talent. It sponsors publications by disadvantaged authors and covers issues that engage wider social concerns. Arkbound fully embraces sustainability and environmental protection. It endeavours to use material that is renewable, recyclable or sourced from sustainable forest.

Arkbound
Backfields House
Upper York Street
Bristol BS2 8QJ
England

www.arkbound.com

"Who are you to judge the life I live? I'm not perfect and don't claim to be! Before you start pointing fingers, make sure your hands are clean."

Bob Marley

Foreword

This book is a difficult read as it relays some very disturbing events and reveals some uncomfortable truths about how individuals, families and society all play a part in people becoming homeless.

Stuart has sensitively assembled a series of stories told by people who have gone through the full range of experiences associated with homelessness. These stories should lead you to reconsider your opinions about this issue. Who is to blame? Is it the individual, their upbringing, their medical and mental health, or social services? More importantly, what can be done about it? Hopefully the conclusions you come to may inspire you to take action or may justify your inaction. That is your choice, but at least you will have thought about it and that is the purpose of this book.

The activities of such charities as First Stop Darlington are about giving these unfortunate people a choice, a support mechanism which will help them overcome their difficulties and will provide them with opportunities for a better life. The stories depict successes and failures, positive outcomes and tragic endings but they all carry a message of hope; that every human life is worth fighting for, whatever the circumstances.

John Kilgour
Chair of Trustees
First Stop Darlington

Prologue

This book is not meant to present an analysis of the causes of homelessness in Darlington, at least not in its entirety. Rather, it attempts to highlight the experiences of some of our most challenging clients who have been brave enough to share their stories and experiences in order to allow you, the reader, to better understand the reality and the causes of homelessness.

The reasons why so many people do not have adequate shelter and lack the skills to live independently are complex, and new insights and explanations emerge with every story told. Homelessness is often the result of a combination of events and problems; some problems are short-term, but many are rooted in long-term issues and behaviours stemming from the homeless person's formative years.

Many feel frustrated at the fact that the number of homeless people seems to be increasing and wonder what can be done to help. Unfortunately, there are no quick fixes or single-remedy solutions. Clearing our streets of rough sleepers may be cosmetically appealing but the real solutions lie in sensitive and often long-term support and rehabilitation.

Take a mixture of mental health problems, family breakdown, erratic school attendance, low educational achievements and learning difficulties, followed by almost inevitable consequences such as minimal skills, poor job prospects, abusive relationships and loss of confidence, and you will start to appreciate some of the problems many vulnerable people have.

There are, of course, services such as our own that allow people who have found themselves homeless the opportunity to turn their lives around by being supportive, enabling and encouraging them to make informed choices. Many of the people with whom we work very often find us as the last stop as other services have found their chaotic lifestyles too much for their own respective agencies to cope with.

To fully understand homelessness you would need to hear the story of every homeless individual. This book offers you seven very real individual experiences of homelessness, each with a story to share and the hope that this may go some way to change many people's perceptions of homelessness.

Of course homelessness won't just disappear, but creating an understanding of the factors that lie behind the real issues is a starting point.

We have tried to recreate events, locales and conversations from my memories of them. In order to maintain their anonymity, in some instances I have changed the names of individuals and places. I may also have changed some identifying characteristics and details such as physical properties, occupations and places of residence. Please note that these case studies are based on interviews and the language used reflects their life experiences.

Clive's Story

As with all stories contained in this book, it's important to understand why Clive has lived his life in the way he has chosen. He recalled his earliest childhood memories.

"I grew up with my mam, three sisters and two brothers in County Durham. I was considered a naughty child when I was very young and I lived up to that tag. I was an angry child," he said. This often manifested itself in violent ways: "Even at less than ten years of age I already had a wild streak, mainly due to boredom, and I got myself involved in all sorts."

Clive felt the fact that his father played no part in his childhood was a contributory factor although, he said, "I'm not sure whether it would have made any difference or whether I'd have done many of the things I did whether he had been in my life or not.

"I really didn't enjoy school very much and would often skip lessons," he said. "Adults were keen for me to attend despite my reluctance to go. My solution was simple. I went up to the school with a friend acting as lookout and when I knew it was unoccupied, I burnt it down. This was one of several 'bad things' I did, but violence and rage were a driving force within me at this time," he explained.

Clive's behaviour became increasingly problematic and concerning for those around him and at thirteen, he was placed in a secure unit.

"This was mainly to assess whether I was a risk to the public – which I was at that time," Clive recalled.

By the age of sixteen, Clive was a contradiction on many levels. He was already estranged from his family but managing to hold down a tenancy, while also holding parties most weekends as well as stealing cars for the "buzz".

Showing a remarkable aptitude for learning, Clive said, "I basically taught myself how to drive while taking cars". His first experience was when, he said, an older "friend" handed him a set of keys and a full tank of petrol which, unsurprisingly, he was unable to resist.

Clive remained responsible enough to pay his rent and basic bills thus maintaining his tenancy, despite being diagnosed with anxiety and depression and already claiming sickness benefit. Clive said his GP was giving him anti-depressants which, he freely admitted, he was not taking regularly, thus making them significantly less effective. He was still in touch with his mother but said he was in such a "dark place" that "she didn't know how to help me".

"I was quite impulsive, so I handed in the keys to my tenancy and returned to County Durham and the family home," he said, and at this point "things began to get much worse".

At the age of seventeen Clive said, "I was introduced to, and began using drugs, when I met a girl who I began a relationship with. I started to explore a cocktail of drugs and basically tried just about every drug going, but heroin became my main problem."

Crime, in particular theft and fraudulent activity, began to intensify in Clive's life as his heroin addiction took hold and the need to feed his habit began to spiral. This reached crisis point for Clive when his mother became so unhappy with his lifestyle that she felt forced to ask him to move out. Yet even then, Clive's life had not reached rock bottom.

"Some of the drugs as well of my state of mind were leading me to commit a number of very violent acts," he recalled.

Clive wasn't specific about the violent acts he committed but he did say that "There were several very violent acts which resulted in hospitalisation for me – and usually those who crossed my path. The final straw for my mother was when she caught sight of my chest slashed wide open, inflicted by one of many people I fought with."

Clive added that his mother was probably also scared he might inflict physical harm to her partner who was living in the family home and whom Clive admitted he resented and had "zero respect" for. Clive said simply, "I was out of control and hated the fact she chose him over me."

Clive acknowledged that he was a troubled young man trying to escape but unsure what he was trying to escape from. On leaving his mother's home Clive became homeless and began resorting to sleeping wherever he could, usually "drug houses" or squats where he would share his drugs in order to have somewhere to stay that night, just to "survive". When this was not an option, Clive said he would break into sheds or, in worst cases, sleep in doorways.

After a cycle of drug use, criminal activity and gratuitous violence, Clive admitted he was unable to maintain the lifestyle he had created, especially without a roof over his head and the breakup from his then girlfriend. Clive was still only nineteen years old.

"I needed some stability in my life at that point and reached out to my sister in County Durham," he asserted.

This was quite hard for both Clive and his sister for very different reasons. He said, "My pride was an issue," but his sister, he said, "Had to get past the fact I'd stolen from her more than once. I was looking quite gaunt and thin, and she became very emotional once she had seen my health had become so bad."

He felt she helped him "heal" as staying with her stabilised him and allowed him the opportunity give his body a rest and come off heroin. Despite this, Clive kept using other drugs, which he justified in his own mind. This meant his lifestyle became incompatible with another member of his family in addition to his mother.

Clive said, "I didn't think it was fair to her to continue to use drugs so I decided to leave and avoid her having to put me out, especially as she had children living with her."

Clive summed up this period by stating; "It seemed that everyone had a place in life except me."

Although he had nowhere to go, Clive again called on the favours of "friends" where he would "sofa-surf" for a night or two before moving on to the next friend. He eventually ended up in hostel accommodation in County Durham where he continued his destructive lifestyle, which he described as "pratting around with lasses and taking drugs".

Soon afterwards, Clive met a girl who went on to become the mother of his child.

He recalled, "I was now 20 years old and she practically fell pregnant straight away".

Despite being surprised by his girlfriend's pregnancy, Clive said he felt "happy" because it gave him a "connection" but at the same time, he admitted, "I wasn't ready to be a dad".

With the hope that his new family would bring about a positive change in his existence, Clive began to contemplate a life of "normality" by taking up a brick-laying course. His girlfriend came from a "normal hard-working family" and had "no type of criminal past", which made him believe he could finally reach a greater stability in his life. Even so, he admitted "I can't really say I even loved her, I just felt an obligation to her as she was pregnant with my child".

This dream of a normal life, however, was short-lived as Clive's criminal acts continued. He remembered how he and a number of "friends" were gathered in their home planning to "tax the local drug dealer" when his girlfriend came back to discover Clive with an array of weapons which, he said, "Shocked her senses". He knew that the best option was to move away from County Durham to prevent his life spiraling out of control even further.

"The police wanted me out of the area as I was committing so much crime," he said. "I was keeping them busy on a daily basis."

Clive's was eventually bailed for an assault on his girlfriend, though this wasn't before they tried a "few more times" to rekindle the relationship. He said, "I didn't want to be with her anymore, I was just passing the time. I knew at that point it wouldn't last".

Clive was now around 21 and his "luck" finally ran out when he was jailed for the first time. He recalled the fateful day that led to his prison sentence.

"I had a long-running feud with the local drug dealer that escalated into another violent encounter. He became racist towards the friend I was with and I kicked the shit out of him, hitting him with several roof tiles and a baseball bat."

Clive admits the beating he dished out was so severe there was only one outcome he could expect. He was promptly given an eighteen month custodial sentence as he accepted a plea deal that spared his friend jail time.

Clive said despite his prison sentence things didn't change much for him, as he has "Struggled to know how to move on with my life even up to today".

Clive's struggles to reform his destructive lifestyle have been difficult as, he admits, "Five prison sentences and remands are hard to argue with".

"When I came out of prison I decided I wanted to make a life for myself in Darlington," he recalled. "Coming to Darlington changed my life – but it was more of an accident as a friend living in Darlington suggested I 'try my luck' with the a housing project based there which luckily had vacancies and were prepared to give me a chance of gaining some stability in life."

He then began to familiarize himself with services in the town and says First Stop soon became a significant source of support in helping him gain some control over his life.

Moving to Darlington was an easy decision. County Durham's local authority was unwilling to house him and he had various ASBOs against his name. In addition, his relationship with his child's mother was over so, as he said, "Being in Darlington was the best option at that time as it meant I would still be close enough to Durham to see my son".

Although Clive was trying hard to get his life in order, there were still "bumps in the road". He was imprisoned a few more times for various things - theft, violence, and street robbery - over the next few years; but after the last sentence ended in February 2013, he said, "I had an epiphany and I realised I was in real danger of completely wasting my life and totally losing contact with my son".

"The thought of losing my liberty scared the shit out of me," he said. He considered the fact that he could continue to be a "career criminal" and that his offences might escalate to "more serious crimes".

"I was scared I might seriously hurt someone or they would seriously hurt me, or worse still end up dead or have a death on my conscience with the lifestyle I was living," he admitted. "There were stories going around the town suggesting I was going to be shot or stabbed so I knew I had to change things in my life".

Upon release from prison, he said, "I'd lost my local connection to Darlington and was homeless, sofa-surfing, sleeping rough and trying to survive".

The memory of seeing close friends overdosing and on two occasions dying also spurred Clive on to change. "I was regularly attending First Stop Darlington at this point and the staff played a big part in helping me at this point," he said.

He recalled meeting his partner, Jenny, who significantly changed his life and his view on relationships.

"I first met Jenny from just seeing her around Darlington. Over time she became a good friend initially, supporting and encouraging me and even rough- sleeping with me."

Clive was, coincidentally, offered accommodation in the very hostel Jenny had moved out of the day before. This was just the thing Clive needed at the time; over the twelve-month period he resided there, his life slowly began to pick up and his criminal activity diminished greatly. Nonetheless, incidents of violence still occurred occasionally. Clive recalled one such time.

"Someone came into my room at the hostel and tried to rob me. I punched the fuck out of him and he left with claret all over his face," he said. "The staff believed my version of events and were very understanding towards me, letting me stay despite this serious breach of the rules."

Clive credited both the hostel and First Stop with giving him the help, support and encouragement to make the necessary adjustments to his lifestyle that enabled him to move towards a more positive direction.

The Present

Whilst this book was being compiled, Clive had begun to attend church, seeking spiritual enlightenment and had been baptised.

"My faith has grown stronger despite the uncertainty of what the future holds," he said.

Despite several obstacles faced and perhaps against all odds, Clive had managed to maintain a council property for three years and to preserve a relationship with his son, though tenuous. Clive had also recently sought help to address his heroin abuse problem by "facing his demons" and entering another drug rehab. On this topic, he declared: "It's an on-going battle which I know I can win".

Sadly, just before this book came to print, and less than two weeks after his latest drug rehabilitation stay, Clive was found dead from a drug overdose. He was just 30 years of age.

Justin's Story

**"I began my first experience of living on the streets
at the age of twelve."**

Justin describes his childhood as "very violent" and, worse
still, there was no escape from it as the violence came
from both parents. Justin said it was a "relief" when they
finally divorced when he was around ten years old.

"My dad's level of cruelty at times was frightening,"
he remembers. "He once crushed a burger into the carpet
with his foot and made me bend down on the floor to lick
and eat it despite it being covered with the hair from our
dog, Tilly. I thought my mother would be horrified at this
treatment from my dad, but I'll never forget the look on her
face and her cruelly laughing before the dawning
realisation that she didn't give a fuck about me."

"She didn't mind him kicking the shit out of us
every night when he came home pissed," he recalls of his
mum. By "us", Justin refers to himself, his two brothers and
two sisters.

He found out years later that his father had been
what Justin described as "interfering with" his sisters. He
emphasises, "I only found out later in life or I would have
made sure he couldn't have done it again."

"I couldn't get my head around the fact that after
the divorce my mother sent me to live with him knowing
what he was. She seemed to favour my brothers and my
sisters over me. I must have been the only kid who
dreaded the summer holidays, which meant having to
spend time with her."

He felt unwanted by her, and consequently he
adds "she hated me and when she got married again, I
knew I wasn't wanted as she now had a 'new family' with
her new husband".

Subsequently, Justin briefly lived with his father
and his grandmother, but this ended abruptly.

"My father tried to 'interfere' with me, expecting me
to sleep in his bed," he says.

Justin decided living on the street was a more preferable option to being with either parent. He explains, "I began my first experience of living on the streets at the age of twelve."

Justin began spending his nights in public toilets in order to protect himself from the elements. This continued on and off during the times he absconded from the various care homes he was put in.

"I began pilfering and was eventually taken into care because I was obviously unable to take care of myself and my parents didn't care one way or the other."

Justin's resentment at being taken into care was made worse by the fact that he was the only sibling of the five who did not remain in the family home. He was unable to accept the regime he encountered in care and, despite being returned, he absconded from the homes in which he had been placed at every opportunity.

He recalls that "In those days it was either fists or feet", a reference to the violence encountered in care homes at that time. "I didn't have one day without a violent occurrence happening to me."

Justin felt "qualified" to talk about treatment in the juvenile care systems within the North-East at that time as, he says, "I resided in five different care homes in four years."

As a coping mechanism, Justin began to develop violent tendencies himself and was twice sent to a detention centre; on both occasions it was for assaulting a policeman. This continued throughout his formative years, from twelve to sixteen years of age. Justin cited these bouts of aggression as being the catalyst for his habit of violence against others later in life.

He remembers the main acts of brutality in care were dished out by the staff.

"They used to set about you as though they were setting about another man." He adds, "I became one angry kid."

In between care homes, he says, "I was again living on the streets pilfering whatever food I could to survive." He recalls one such time when he sneaked into someone's house to steal an apple pie out of the oven.

In 1982, at the age of sixteen, Justin was released from the detention centre where he had been sent and, as the care system had no further duty, was returned to his father's home.

"They simply dumped me there," he says. "I was back to square one".

Justin was reunited with his father "because there was no alternative option". Remarkably, he stayed with his dad on and off for the next two years while trying to reunite with his estranged mother. Justin said neither experience was particularly successful. He describes those two years simply as "a form of existence".

Reflecting on his childhood, Justin says he became very familiar to both criminal activity and gratuitous violence, which resulted in him being consistently incarcerated, then released – a process that continued throughout his adult life. He admitted he had never really considered accommodation of his own as he had never been out of prison for a prolonged enough period to maintain a tenancy.

"Most of my adult life outside prison has been spent 'sofa-surfing' and relying on people I know to put me up," he admits.

Justin's only recollection of living independently was for a brief time in a bedsit provided by a housing project but, because of his propensity for finding himself in trouble with the police, Justin's tenancy was inevitably short-lived.

His first experience of prison life happened around this time. He explains, "It was water off a duck's back to me because everything that could possibly be done to me had already been done."

Justin's early life was, in his own words, "horrific" and set the tone for his adult life. He says, "I have never known what most people see as a 'normal life' as I've spent the last 30 years in and out of prison." The prison sentences were mostly for violence: "I was rebelling against the system and was involved in prison riots on a few occasions."

Justin did, however, feel his "rage" had diminished over the past few years as he had come to terms and accepted a lot of things that happened in his childhood. He says, "It was a healing process. All that was inside had to come out."

During spells in prison Justin showed his capacity and motivation for self-education and was able to complete two degrees in Law and Sociology, in Wealdstone and Dartmoor prisons respectively.

When asked what Justin wanted for himself in the future he says simply, "I want to wake up without having to worry about catching pneumonia, and without wondering where my next meal is coming from."

The Present

Justin remains "anti-establishment" and has continued to drift in and out of the prison system.

He found himself homeless and roofless at the start of 2016 and on arrest for an unspecified crime, was so cold sleeping out that he asked the judge to jail him for his offence. The judge obliged.

Paula's Story

"This showed me a different way of life, a glimpse of normality. Proper family life for the first time ever."

Though born in England, Paula felt her "roots" were formed in the Mediterranean. She describes her childhood as a "nightmare", involving "several beatings" inflicted by her mother.

Paula's parents split up when she was just two years old. Her mother moved in with another partner and had another child. Reflecting on her mother's history, Paula felt her own life was in some ways a "mirror image" of her mother's.

"When I met my partner, he was physically abusive to me and I thought for a long time that was normal behaviour," she explained. "I thought to show love you had to be physical. He would say to me, 'I've done it because I love you'!"

Paula admitted to being a "difficult and troubled child", describing herself as a "bully and a thief" in her school environment, constantly being expelled, usually for fighting. She was around twelve years old at this point and, although she made no excuses for her behaviour, she explained, "My mother was in prison during this period of my life."

As a consequence of her mother's detention, Paula and her sister were packed off to live with her grandparents.

"Things began to get worse for me," Paula said. "I began to discover other pleasures in life and began smoking and drinking alcohol."

She said she also began "hanging out with the wrong crowd". Some of these "friends" were older than Paula and encouraged her to play truant from school. She said, "I didn't take much persuading because I found being part of an older crowd and being accepted by them was more important to me. I was out of control and too much of a handful for my grandparents."

This continued for nearly two years during which time social services became involved. Before long, however, Paula's mother was released from prison and they were reunited. Far from this being a happy experience, Paula said shortly after her mother's release she ran away.

Paula's mother wanted to lay down some ground rules which she not only resisted but rebelled against. She decided London would be her destination as she set off to find her father. She said, "I knew my dad was living in Essex and decided I wanted to be with him."

She had some details, including an address where he had been living, so she managed to find him and turned up on his doorstep. She said it was the "one and only time" she had spent with him since she was two years of age and had no memory of him up to this point. She reflected, "If I hadn't gone to London I would never have met him."

This didn't last long, as social services were to take a hand and returned Paula to her hometown where, at the age of sixteen, she was promptly placed in a bedsit. Far from struggling here, she thrived: "I was very good at paying my bills and I also enrolled at college in hairdressing."

Paula credits this part of her life as the reason she has always been so independent. She said, "I was on £35.00 a week and back then you could lie to a landlord and get away with it as landlords weren't always so strict with background checks."

Paula managed to maintain her tenancy for eighteen months and, proving a maturity beyond her years, paid all her utilities and bills when they were due.

Despite this, Paula admitted, there were too many temptations to resist for someone of such a tender age and, while still mixing and partying with older girls, she began experimenting with ecstasy and LSD. Inevitably, Paula began to go off the rails. She said all the partying put paid to her college ambitions and her attendance began to drop off until she stopped going altogether. She subsequently lost her tenancy after using money to buy recreational drugs which, she admitted, was "More of a priority than rent and bills".

This period, however, coincided with her meeting a young man who would change her life. At seventeen, while continuing to enjoy herself and party like most young people, Paula met Eric at a nightclub and almost as soon as her tenancy ended, moved into the home Eric shared with his parents.

She said, "They showed me a different way of life, a glimpse of normality. Proper family life for the first time ever."

Ironically, this made Paula dislike and resent her mother even more. She explained, "I saw Eric's mother showing such love to her family and wondered why my mother wasn't like that with me."

Referring to the abusive behaviour of her father towards her mother, Paula stated, "My mother picked up with me where my dad had left off with her." Years later, this was confirmed to Paula by her mother who told her, "You reminded me so much of your dad."

As Paula found herself settled into a loving family environment, she also found herself pregnant. She was nineteen when her daughter, Joanne, was born. Just as Paula started to settle into family life with Eric and their young child, however, she began to see changes in Eric's behaviour. She said, "He began falling asleep, slavering, and was often incoherent. It was obvious to me he had become a serious drug user."

Paula said she had moved away from ecstasy and LSD and was "smoking joints" (cannabis), which Eric began to roll and smoke with her. She recalled, "Within three days, I woke up in agony with flu-like symptoms, physically rattling, realising he had laced my joint with heroin, his drug of choice. Within those three days I was hooked."

One single moment sent Paula's life on a downward spiral which changed her life forever. She was set to become a prolific shoplifter, stealing daily to feed her newly-acquired habit. Paula remembered when she began shoplifting: "I was still trying to be a 'normal mother' and feed and look after my child."

This, however, wasn't compatible with her "other life" as a heroin user. She recalled, "I packed up a little suitcase for my daughter and took her to my mother's house because I knew she would be safe and looked after there. Joanne was now two years old and I tried to explain to her that 'mummy's poorly and has to go to hospital'".

In reality Paula wasn't going to hospital – she was going to prison, as her daily shoplifting activities had caught up with her. The choice of giving her child to her parents was incredible brave; the responsible thing to do, knowing that her court date was fast approaching and having been warned by the solicitor that prison time was unavoidable.

Thinking about things practically Paula added, "I also didn't want social services getting too involved in my daughter's life and wanted minimum disruption for her."

In fact social services did look at her circumstances and decided to allow Paula's daughter to remain with her mother. Paula, for her part, received her first conviction at the age of twenty and was given a twenty eight-day custodial sentence. She confessed, "I sobbed my heart out every day I was there. For a twenty year old serving her first sentence, I found the whole experience terrifying."

Paula did, however, feel that the whole experience was a "blessing in disguise" as, she said, "I was able to do my rattle and come out of prison having cleared my system of all the drugs I'd been using".

Despite doing her "rattle", she began using drugs again immediately after her release. She explained, "I don't know what it is but something calls you back."

She pretty much picked up where she left off before her prison sentence, going straight back to Eric who consequently coaxed and encouraged her to begin shoplifting again: "I didn't stop to think why he had me shoplifting; it wasn't until later when I realised he didn't want to get locked up but didn't mind if I did. I did the shoplifting while he waited outside. There was no risk for him."

Paula was soon caught again, receiving a three-month custodial sentence. Unfortunately, this was to become a regular occurrence in hers.

During this bleak period of her life, her relationship with Eric ended and as a result she lost the loving and stable family life his parents had provided. Paula also had no regular place to live in on her release. She ended up staying with a variety of different people over the many spells she had on leaving prison. She said: "I think over the past twenty years I've probably spent about fourteen in prison." Paula estimated that she has been in prison over twenty times, mainly for shoplifting. The biggest sentence she received was eight years, for robbery.

As the relationship with her daughter became increasingly difficult to maintain, Paula felt a gap developing that grew over time. She recounted, "On one of those the times that I called her from prison she stopped calling me 'mummy' and started calling me 'Paula'."

At the time of her eight-year sentence, which she described as "a true wake-up call", Paula was thirty-one years old and had spent almost as many years in as out of prison. She stated, "The change began when I came out of prison after serving five years of the eight-year sentence I received."

Following her release she relapsed again, getting on "the slippery slope" she relapsed again. But then, Paula said, "I decided to go onto a methadone programme, which was something I had never previously considered."

By now Paula's daughter was twelve years old. She said, "I could see she was getting difficult for my mother to control and that she was becoming more and more like I was at that age. It was at this point I knew I had to pull myself together."

Paula then decided to lay out a plan to get her daughter back and prevent the girl from "going down the same path" as her. She secured her first property since the age of sixteen and achieved her aim to get her daughter returned to her care by maintaining her abstinence. Slowly, she began putting her life together over the next couple of years.

There were unavoidable setbacks. Paula explained, "I had forgotten how to be a mother and struggled to adapt to motherhood in the same way as my daughter struggled to cope with living with me after ten years of staying with my mum. I had a support worker at that time who proved invaluable; she used to help me with my bills and budgeting as I'd often get into a panic when trying to sort things on my own."

Despite Paula's attempts to become a stable influence in her daughter's life, by the time she was fourteen or fifteen, Joanne had started smoking and drinking and doing exactly what Paula had done at the same age. Her worst fears had come true.

Paula tried to instill some discipline into her daughter by revoking her pocket money and grounding her, but to no avail. Her daughter's rebellious streak continued and gradually worsened. Paula recalled, "She began to take amphetamines and ended up in hospital for three days."

Soon after this Joanne began assaulting her mother, saying, "I'm going to make your life a living nightmare." Paula admitted, "I let her smash up my house, I let her physically attack me without defending myself - once she even broke my nose - because she needed to get that previous hurt and rejection out."

She confessed, "I had feelings of guilt because of spending so much of her childhood separated from her. I would always say to my daughter that 'nothing is so bad that you can't tell me'. So together, after a lot of soul-searching and tears, we managed to deal with it."

Paula admitted to resorting to devious methods initially: "I used to follow her and make sure she wasn't hanging out with the people who had sold her drugs. I even went to the police, encouraging them to take the door off the property she was visiting as there were other younger children living in this property where drugs were being sold."

Paula said her instincts were proved right: "The children were taken into care and the drug dealer was eventually jailed, but it also meant I got my daughter back."

On her childhood and its bearing on her present life, she reflected, "My mother has never been able to verbally express herself and tell me how much I'm loved. I was determined to break that cycle and show my daughter how much she's loved – and I did."

Paula's new-found happiness wasn't to last, however, and before long, finding herself short of money, she began to "slip", using heroin again and resorting to shoplifting to support her drug habit. Meanwhile, Paula's daughter became pregnant at a time that coincided with her mother's sentencing for a further offence.

The Present

Paula continues to "bounce" in and out of the prison system. She is now a grandmother of two with the birth of her third grandchild imminent and continues to battle against her heroin addiction. She is currently attending a local drug service where she has just gone back onto a methadone programme.

Paula has also just moved into her first stable tenancy in several years. She maintains a healthy relationship with her daughter.

Martin's Story

"I was eating pizza off pavements."

Martin's early years were far from ideal. "Memorable," he stated, "but not in a positive sense. "When I was young, I remember my mam suffered from MS and my dad worked away on the rigs."

Martin's dad returned home but, Martin said, "He was an alcoholic and he was very abusive to us which was obviously hard to live with."

Martin lived in the family home with his mum, dad, brother and sister and recalled those early days, saying, "My dad used to go out to the pub and return very drunk and, for no apparent reason, used to start hitting us." He felt powerless throughout his childhood, but his father's actions also left him angry. These feelings changed Martin from a happy-go-lucky child to someone who became "deeply troubled".

Martin described the first time he achieved a measure of revenge on his father: "When I was twenty-one he came home one day drunk, as usual, and wanting to throw his weight around. On this occasion he got more than he bargained for – I hit him. This was the first time I was locked up, but it was worth it."

Martin felt that this age was significant for another reason: "I came home one day and found my mother had gone. Her bags were gone and so was she. I found out that she had been taken into protective care. There had only been me and my parents living in the family home—my brother and sister had already left because they were unable able to cope with my dad's abuse any longer."

Martin said although he was relatively young, he was responsible for paying all the bills that came into the house. He recalled the day his father also finally left the family home.

"It was a Wednesday teatime," he said, when his father announced simply, "I'm moving out on Friday."

This was significant for Martin because with his mother in protective care, his father giving up the family home and Martin himself having little contact with his siblings, he found himself alone and about to be made homeless.

Martin explained, "My dad was an alcoholic and had previously sold the property then rented it back to fund his drinking habit. I felt rejected by both my parents." He said of his father, "I can't stand him".

Martin described his first experience of homelessness: "I just felt lost. I didn't know what to do or where to go. Luckily," he said, "I became aware of services that offered support."

Through a friend, and in desperation, Martin turned to First Stop Darlington to help him try to secure a tenancy. In turn he was referred to a housing project in the town which, fortunately, had vacancies. Martin stayed for six months before finding himself in another supported accommodation where he stayed for nine months before moving into Salvation Army housing for a further year. Martin admitted to "bouncing around from one place to another for two to three years", with little thought of a permanent home.

He said at this time there was zero contact with his mum or dad or any of his siblings, adding, "I was as interested in them as they were in me."

After "messing up" his tenancy at the Salvation Army, losing it by "breaking the rules," Martin found himself homeless. He said, "This was the worst possible time to lose a tenancy and become homeless as it was winter time". Martin said that at no point did he ever even consider turning to his family as "they wouldn't have cared anyway".

"I had no money and there were periods of heavy snow that winter. All I had was a sleeping bag and a coat. I was eating pizza off pavements that people had discarded. I couldn't claim benefits at that time because I was of no fixed abode and didn't have a care of address."

Martin recounted scavenging in bins for food many times. He said, "Saturday nights were always good as pizza, kebab, and the odd few quid could be had from people in the town, who were more generous when they were drunk. There were other people though who would shout obscenities, spit at me or kick me just for being homeless. I sometimes found shelter under a nearby railway bridge where I often stayed that winter as it would protect me from the wind and rain."

Sadly, Martin spent many nights – almost a year - in these harsh conditions. Describing this time as simply "surviving", he said, "I lost count of the amount of times I ended up fighting, forced to protect myself after being picked on for being homeless." Martin explained, and he found this somewhat ironic, "The police kept giving me hassle because I used to drink to keep warm and all they saw was a drunken man lying around."

Understandably, Martin's health suffered from these conditions and his weight plummeted from fifteen stone to just a little over eight stone. He admitted it was at this point that he found a comfort in and fondness of alcohol and started drinking heavily. Staying sober, he said, has been "a long and continuous battle lasting over seven years", with several periods of abstinence and then relapse.

He said, "My life had turned to shit and I knew I had to try to change how I was living or I would end up dead." Having made that decision, Martin approached First Stop in 2010.

"It turned out to be a good decision as they were able to get me into a bed and breakfast in Darlington temporarily," he said. "That first night's sleep was the best night's sleep I've ever had."

This triggered a change in fortune as he was then able to access benefits again, thus receiving enough money to buy essentials. Martin's time living on the street, however, left him suffering with both anxiety and depression as a consequence of his homeless existence and it was then that he was referred to hospital in order to address his mental state.

Martin's alcohol intake was still rising, after a breakup which Martin described as "devastating at the time". The alcohol was a coping mechanism as well as an addiction. Martin said, "The drinking became the trigger for all of my relationship breakdowns, including with my family."

After a few months of living in temporary accommodation, Martin was able to access a private rented two-bedroom property which, despite his battle with alcoholism, he was able to maintain. He felt the turning point was "having the balls to accept as much help as I could from different services". Among the services Martin accessed were an accommodation service, First Stop Darlington, hospital services (CPN support) and drug and alcohol services, all of which, he said, had greatly helped him over the past twelve years.

Martin remained on anti-depressants, to cope with his anxiety, and maintained visits with drug and alcohol services to help him address his alcohol addiction. Nevertheless, he managed to keep his tenancy.

He said of his family, "I haven't had a relationship with my brother and sister since I was twenty-one (for over twelve years) and although I've tried to make contact with my dad he never answers his door... I've tried but he's just not bothered."

Poignantly, Martin said, "I just want to be normal and get off the drink or I know I'll be dead by Christmas."

The Present

Despite Martin's constant battle against alcohol addiction, he eventually lost his fight for life in early 2016, due to sclerosis of the liver, aged just 33. Sadly, he remained at odds with his family.

Gina's Story

"I was running away from the care homes at regular intervals, and sleeping in derelict buildings."

Gina was brought up on a council estate with her parents and her two sisters. She described her childhood as "horrific".

"You think your dad is going to be there to protect you from the world. My father began abusing me in childhood from the age of four up to the age of fourteen, both physically and sexually. It still impacts my life today."

She explained, "I found myself skiving off school quite a lot and I rebelled against everything. The only time I had to be by myself was when I was supposed to be at school. I was running away from school and home a lot although my mother wasn't aware of why. She put me in care assuming I was just a problem child."

Gina was in care from the age of thirteen until she was sixteen. This was complicated by the fact she was moved around without any stability at that time and being estranged from her siblings only added to her feeling of isolation. She said, "I was running away from the care homes at regular intervals, and sleeping in derelict buildings."

Gina remembered one such experience: "I ran away (again), hitchhiking to Blackpool when I was fourteen before making my way to Liverpool for no other reason than to get away. I was totally oblivious to the dangers that came with it. There was another time when I hitchhiked to Blackpool and was picked up by a much older man who asked for my underwear in exchange for money."

Running away would always end in a similar fashion for Gina; "the police would eventually PNC me [which gives access to information on police national databases] and I'd be taken back to my captors."

Understandably, Gina harboured feelings of bitterness and anger not only towards her father but also her mother as she felt "abandoned" when she was put into care. This also had lifelong effect on Gina's relationship with her sisters, especially her middle sister who she described as a "daddy's girl". This sibling refused to accept anything "negative" said about their father even though Gina said, "We were all abused, but she doesn't remember things in the same detail or the same way I do".

Gina described her relationship with this sister as "very fractured" although, she said, "I love her and would always be there for her if anything happened."

On leaving care aged sixteen, Gina didn't return to the family home as she felt this was never an option, despite the fact that her father was sentenced and jailed the previous year, when the abuse Gina described came to light. Instead she moved into a guest house with an older friend; this was her first experience of independent living.

Perhaps unsurprisingly, this wasn't a total success as Gina's older friend was twenty-three and moved on relatively quickly after being offered her own tenancy. Being left alone Gina struggled financially as she had become reliant on splitting the utility bills with her friend; having to survive by herself was a huge responsibility for a sixteen-year-old.

Gina said living independently helped her develop certain life skills from an early age which stood her in good stead in later life: "I was able to develop skills in budgeting, cooking and generally maintaining a home, which I was surprisingly better at than I'd expected."

Gina became reunited with her friend and stayed in a relatively secure arrangement with her for two years before meeting a man, Wayne, who would eventually become her husband. She was still just seventeen years old when she met her new partner, who, unbeknown to Gina, was a former heroin addict.

Gina became acquainted with the drug. She said, "I had never even given a thought to heroin at that point in my life. He was also taking speed, which he told me about probably thinking I wouldn't see that as a major issue. He made it sound okay and I eventually began to take speed with him".

It was only later she began to realise he was disappearing into the kitchen to inject it. Gina recounted, "We were painting the house one night and as he rolled up his sleeves, I noticed needle tracks in his arms which I asked him about. He was at least being honest with me admitting he was injecting. I was very much against injecting anything and really struggled to accept this revelation."

She cited that experience as the start of her descent into drug-taking: "One day someone turned up at the house we now shared, saying they had 'found' a heroin stash and knew that Wayne had enough contacts to be able to sell it on, so they asked him if he wanted to buy it. He brought the entire stash, selling half of it and keeping the other half for his own personal use."

He continued to "coax, cajole and encourage" Gina to try it and eventually persuaded her to "give it a try" by telling her it was the last time he was ever going to have heroin. "So I did," she admitted. Gina was just seventeen years old, with a boyfriend significantly older than her; however, she offered no excuses for using drugs.

Gina began smoking it and said of her first experience, "I hated it; I couldn't lift my head up and I kept being sick. It was awful."

Gina acknowledged that the relationship was "destructive" in many ways, especially health-wise. She said, "We both went back to injecting speed, not just occasionally but every day."

In addition, both Gina and her partner began to "enjoy" a lot of cannabis which was also becoming a daily habit. Gina described this part of her life as "lost years" and a bit of a "haze". This began a cycle that lasted for three years and only ended when Gina became pregnant with her first child at nineteen.

She realised that to continue using would potentially have serious consequences for her unborn child and decided to stop her drug consumption. She admitted this was "incredibly difficult" as she was still living with Wayne who had absolutely no intention of quitting his drug use. There were arguments as a result and he was often violent towards her: "He once dragged me over the back field when I was pregnant and hit me. We were heading towards the river. He had a knife in his hand and I was on my knees begging for my life. I really thought that was it for me, I thought he was going to kill me. I managed to convince him that I wasn't going to leave him and he eventually calmed down."

Her concerns were justified as Gina learned his violent episodes were not just directed at her. She said, "He had fractured a lad's skull with an iron bar and assaulted another man by breaking his arm with a baseball bat."

Far from this being a wakeup call for Gina, however, she saw this as normality and said this had zero effect on her relationship with him at that time. She recalled, "I had a violent dad who used to beat me and a partner that did the same. It was what I knew life to be like with a male presence in it."

A significant event soon after the birth of her child brought about the end of the relationship, though. Gina said, "He went to hit me and ended up hitting our son. That was a step too far and I immediately ended the relationship."

This decision was short-lived though, as before too long, Gina confessed, "I took him back not once but twice." After the second occasion Gina became pregnant again at the age of twenty-one. If she felt things might change at that point, she was wrong. "The abuse just carried on until my first child was around eighteen months old when I finally split up with Wayne permanently," she said.

Despite her damaging relationship, Gina said, "I jumped straight into another relationship. I absolutely hated being on my own." Her new partner, Kevin, was working away in Germany but on his return, two months later, Gina began living with him and ended up moving in, along with her two children. This was a complicated arrangement as Kevin was in the process of buying his ex-wife out of the house when he met Gina. She described him as "the total opposite of Wayne and way too soft with me".

Gina said, "I needed someone to say 'no' to me sometimes and my new partner just wasn't like that. He was working so he was giving me money all the time thinking he was helping me but I was spending it as fast as he was giving it to me. Kevin eventually lost his job because of me."

She explained, "I ended up calling him at work - he was working in Middlesborough at the time - begging him to go and score me some drugs and come back home with them. He would be leaving work regularly, often in the middle of the day. What employer is going to put up with someone disappearing in the middle of the day?"

Despite the fact that Gina was still struggling to address her addiction, she remained in the relationship and became pregnant with her third child. She was still only twenty-five years old.

Gina said, "I decided to address my addiction and went to a treatment service, which enabled me to get onto a methadone programme."

Her third child was born prematurely but healthy, though needing time in a special care baby unit. Despite the "relief" of having a new baby born healthy, Gina began to use heroin again shortly after giving birth. Things were beginning to spiral out of control. Gina said, "My drug use had taken over my life big style. After his sacking, Kevin still wasn't working and we were that much in debt that we ended up losing the house, two cars, and a caravan, all of which he had previously bought outright."

Gina somehow managed to keep things together enough to move into a council house along with Kevin and her three boys. She explained, "This was the trigger I needed to get my life back on track."

Gina decided to put her time to more productive use by setting up an IT contracting business in order to build a better life for herself, her partner and her sons. "Kevin had already had experience in this area so it wasn't as difficult a transition as it might have been," she said.

Despite having made great strides to reform her life, Gina maintained a drug habit, which she felt was due in part to moving into a council estate well known to her, meaning she began "knocking about with a girl who was heavily into drugs". Not only did Gina's heroin habit escalate again, but her new "friend" introduced her to other drugs, specifically "crack".

Shortly after, Gina began cashing cheques out of the business account as she was now company director and had unlimited access to the business finances. She explained, "I used to forge Kevin's signature as it needed two names on the cheque. It would be £1,000 here, £500 there and meant I could easily afford my heroin, crack cocaine and alcohol addictions."

Gina freely admitted, "I was just totally and utterly out of control. I was using more than I ever had previously and was spending several hundred pounds a week on a cocktail of drugs."

Unsurprisingly, Gina lost the business which went bust. Consequently, she decided then to try to address her drug use once more by going into detox, where she was put on a naltrexone programme. She said, "They put me to sleep, then woke me up on the third day, gave me Naltrexone and I went back to sleep. They then woke me up on day five and kicked me out. I was still withdrawing and feeling really poorly because they had given me a blocker - I was really violently ill: vomit, diarrhoea, the lot."

Once Gina had returned home she found handprints between her legs which, she said, could only have happened when she was in detox.

"After discussion with Kevin, I decided not to take it any further, despite speaking to them about it. Their explanation was they had to put me in the shower to wash me and I'd been struggling, so we just left it at that. But the handprint to me didn't make sense. It would have made more sense if it was perhaps the back of my legs, but I don't know and I try not to think about it, to be honest."

As soon as Gina was back on her feet, she admitted, "I went out and ended up scoring heroin despite the fact it made me really poorly. It had me in its grip, I simply couldn't stop. Kevin then gave me an ultimatum, 'stop using or I'll start using too'."

She said, "I tried to stop but I couldn't, so he stuck to his word and started using. I think he did it because he thought my love for him would make me stop and think, but I just didn't have the strength of will to resist. It became too much trying to support two habits continually smoking so we both began to inject heroin."

Kevin became addicted really quickly, which, Gina said, was consistent with his personality. This became a major problem as they simply could not maintain a lifestyle of constant drug use with no income. Their need for heroin became increasingly desperate and Gina was arrested for shoplifting with her children in tow – an experience made even worse by one of the children telling his friends at school that he had been in jail with his mummy. "I felt really ashamed," Gina admitted.

Inevitably this led to social services intervention. Gina recalled, "They told me that morning there would be no way they would be taking the kids, that it would be just an informal meeting and there would be no need for a solicitor. I got to the meeting and they had asked the social worker to take the kids to the park. They then asked my mum and Kevin's mum if they were able to take the kids, which they were until they could get them into a foster placement."

This period, which Gina described as the worst of her life, coincided with Kevin being arrested trying to shoplift for the first time. Gina said, "I actually tried to kill myself. We were due to meet up at a pre-arranged time and place and he didn't turn up so I got in a taxi to go home from the town. I knew I had no money to pay for it. When I got in the taxi I saw the driver's money bag in the side of the door. I picked it up without him noticing and when he pulled up to where I asked, near an alleyway I knew well, I legged it.

I bought gear with the £120 I had stolen. I knew Kevin would need some gear when he came out of the police station so I saved him a £10 bag and put the rest of the gear on a spoon, sat on my son's bed and tried to kill myself, but the gear I'd bought was crap. It should have been enough to put me over, but it wasn't."

Gina reflected on that episode of her life for several seconds before asserting that this was definitely the lowest point in her life. After losing her children, the loss of her home quickly followed. "I was just taking gear, gear and more gear. That was all I thought about from morning to night. I had stopped paying my rent and didn't even consider paying bills."

Pretty soon Gina acquired significant rent arrears and was unceremoniously evicted with Kevin. Unable to find any friends willing to house two people with a serious drug addiction, they were forced to live on the street. Gina said, "It was torture. It was winter and the weather temperature was freezing. We were almost blue with cold.

"I reached out to my mum, who although sympathetic to my situation, wouldn't put me up. I don't blame her for that, remembering the state I was in. I became very reliant on First Stop Darlington at the time, as they allowed me to use their facilities for showers and the laundry to wash the few clothes I had left. By my recollection, I spent eight months living on the street, sleeping in abandoned buildings, in shop doorways or anywhere that provided shelter from the cold and rain."

Finally Gina and Kevin were placed into a bed and breakfast by the local council, accommodation which, according to Gina, "was only one step up from the streets and was in an absolutely disgusting condition". It did allow the pair to get their lives back together but shortly after leaving the bed and breakfast, their relationship finally ended when Kevin began to show signs of violence towards Gina. She described one incident just prior to the breakup: "After a very trivial spat, he had hold of my head and actually put it through a telephone kiosk window."

Gina ended that relationship immediately but jumped straight into another, not realising that she was already pregnant with her fourth child. She was twenty-seven-years-old.

The positive thing, according to Gina, was that her new partner was no pushover. She explained, "He was a lot stronger with me. He stood up to me and said 'no' to me; by being so forceful, he actually managed to help me."

Gina realised she would have to address her drug use before she would be considered stable enough to get access to her children. With the support of her new partner, Nigel, she began to attend a drug treatment centre where she was put on a methadone programme.

It wasn't plain sailing, however, and Gina struggled to give clean samples. After three negative samples though, she was able to take her methadone home fortnightly. She said, "This turned out to be a blessing in disguise as Nigel was able to pick it up and would measure the methadone out into smaller bottles and police my daily use."

Gina was on 80mg of methadone at that point but she said, "Unbeknown to me, every three or four days he would reduce my methadone by two or three milligrams. I eventually realised what he was doing but agreed for him to continue and I eventually got it down to 10mgs."

Gina had addressed her drug use significantly shortly before giving birth to her fourth son, Jacob, at the age of twenty-eight.

Because of her previous issues, Jacob was immediately taken from her and put into foster care. This was a particularly difficult time for Gina because she was doing everything to address her drug and housing issues, while at the same time having her three eldest children put up for adoption and her new child taken into care.

With Nigel's help, however, Gina was able to stop the proposed adoption process, proving she was now drug free and leading a stable life. Gina began to seek some independence and, though still in a relationship with Nigel, she eventually found herself a house of her own, enabling her to regain custody of her four children.

Unfortunately for Gina, her previous partner reappeared and began to cause her problems by asking to see the children, which wasn't allowed as he was still using. Gina explained, "Even though I was giving negative samples, Kevin told social services that I was using and dealing drugs, which was enough for them to take my children off me again while they investigated his claim."

Ironically, this triggered Gina to start using again after moving back in with Nigel. Before long, at the age of twenty-eight, Gina was pregnant again with her fifth child. Just before Christmas Eve, at twenty-four weeks, Gina delivered her stillborn child, which she described as "heart breaking for both of us".

By the following year, Gina was pregnant for the sixth time, eventually giving birth to a daughter, Alice, but again her happiness was short-lived. After checking his safe, Nigel realised a significant amount of money was missing and, not waiting for an explanation, threw Gina out of the house at 2am. She said, "I don't know why he decided to check it at that time in the morning as I had stolen it about ten days before."

Her daughter was just eight months old. Nigel had promised Gina he would return Alice once she could demonstrate she had a stable family home but Gina was now homeless again.

The Present

Gina has continued to live her life in the same way over the intervening years. She has managed to avoid prison, despite admitting to numerous offences and deliberately trying to "sabotage" her own life.

She is in stable private rented accommodation and still "slipping occasionally" by using heroin. She is currently on another methadone programme and expressed a desire to explore rehab again.

She is also in a relationship with her new partner and despite an ongoing battle to try and get her children back, Gina still does not have full custody of any of her children.

Ronnie's Story

"I went on the run because my addiction meant I owed money to people and my life had begun to unravel and spiral out of control."

Ronnie's story began twenty-seven years ago in Birkenhead on the Wirral. He recalled his early childhood memories as "memorable for all the wrong reasons".

He said, "I was taken into care at the age of eleven and remained there till I was sixteen after being physically and emotionally abused by my dad. As mum decided to stay with him, my relationship with her ended then."

This had other repercussions for Ronnie as he was separated from his older brother and was never again to share a home with his only sibling, although they did "reconnect" and speak from time to time later in life.

Ronnie was taken into care in the Lake District which he described as quite "scary". He said, "I didn't know anybody and felt intimidated by the older kids in those early days." After a while, things began to change, though not necessarily for the better, as Ronnie no longer felt intimidated by the other children but started to get into fights with them.

"School was hard: I was picked on and bullied during my school years and, as I was quiet for the most part, it allowed other kids to carry on bullying me," he said. "I tried to tell the so-called professionals, teachers and care staff about being bullied but this fell on deaf ears and little or nothing was done to address my torment."

At the age of sixteen Ronnie went to what he describes as a respite college in Birmingham which, he said, was very similar to a hostel and had educational facilities. The project helped young people to develop essential life skills, which enabled them to become semi-independent, preparing them for their first-time tenancies.

Ronnie explained, "This was a valuable experience in my personal development but was also a negative as I was moving away from all the things familiar to me from my childhood. It was a difficult transition and meant I had to start all over again. It took me a long time to get to build other relationships, especially as I was so quiet and withdrawn."

This was only supposed to be for a couple of years but Ronnie stayed until he was twenty-five, a total of nine years. He reflected, "I guess as I kept my head down and didn't cause any trouble they continued to review my position yearly and offer me an extension year on year."

As the "cut-off age" was twenty-five, Ronnie was not able to stay beyond this time and was given help to adjust to being on his own for the first time in his life. This coincided with a "dark period" for him as his mental health became "fragile" and his situation only worsened when he began to take drugs; indeed, this created a vicious cycle, with Ronnie shoplifting in order to feed the cocaine and speed habit he had acquired.

Before he could even address his impending housing issue, Ronnie admitted, "I went on the run because my addiction meant I owed money to people and my life had begun to unravel and spiral out of control."

Ronnie says that this period was the most testing time he had ever experienced. He found himself rough sleeping, "usually in large metal refuse bins with black rubbish bin bags acting as a mattress".

By this time Ronnie had moved around, living in various cities across the country as he searched for somewhere he could call "home". He eventually found himself in Sheffield.

He recalled, "I relied on the kindness of strangers for money so at least I could eat most days. On the rare days I didn't have money I would steal food to survive. If I couldn't steal I'd eat people's leftover food that I'd come across."

This experience continued for several months before Ronnie decided to seek medical help. In consultation with his doctor, Ronnie realised that his mental health had deteriorated badly; he had considered harming either himself or someone else. He was voluntarily admitted to hospital, where he remained for several months while he addressed his mental health issues.

On his release from the hospital, he moved into a hostel in Sheffield, which he left after a year to continue his itinerant lifestyle; nonetheless, he kept gaining access to mental health services, in particular those services meant for vulnerable adults who wish to live semi-independently without settling in one place.

Present Day

Ronnie has continued to live an itinerant lifestyle, staying in several bed and breakfast establishments across Darlington. He has spoken about his ambitions to go to college and fulfil his passion to become a chef.

He continues to suffer from anxiety and depression, and is still fighting an ongoing battle to become drug free. Ronnie has had no contact for several years with either of his parents and is not sure whether they are dead or alive. Sadly, he has lost contact with his brother.

However, he has recently developed a loving relationship and moved into his first stable home with his partner, hoping for what he describes as "a normal life".

Emma's Story

"I was sleeping in the graveyard behind the back of Wilkinson's"

Emma was brought up in the North-East of England and described her formative years as being "normal to me". She explained, "My earliest memories were my mum and dad regularly arguing, splitting up and getting back together. My mum was an alcoholic and they just couldn't live together for any length of time. The consequences were I had to look after my brother who was six years younger than me as my mum was always drunk."

Emma was extremely resentful of her mother's actions. She said, "Because I had to look after my little brother I wasn't allowed to have a normal childhood; I had to stay home most days and be responsible for him, making sure he was alright."

It was of little surprise then that Emma became involved with the wrong crowd at school; and, she admitted, "When I was twelve years old I began sniffing glue and generally rebelling against everything and everyone."

Such behaviour appears to have stemmed from Emma's difficult relationship with her mother: "I really hated my mum and this was the main reason I left home by the age of fifteen."

With little or no parental supervision or guidance, Emma soon showed an interest in boys and at the age of sixteen she became pregnant. Back then Emma was living with an older girl she used to babysit for: "She gave me a place to stay which was more of a stable environment than living with my parents."

Emma met her boyfriend as he lived just around the corner. Smiling at the memory, she said, "He used to walk up and down the street all the time trying to get my attention."

When Emma realised she was pregnant - just two months after they met - she also discovered her boyfriend was the local drug dealer, which resulted in Emma's introduction to drugs: "He made me try amphetamine, which I thought was great as I had previously been very quiet and withdrawn and this gave me the confidence I had lacked."

Emma said she came to her senses shortly after giving birth. After just four months Emma decided to cut her losses and split up from her boyfriend. She said, "I had been suffering a lot of domestic violence from him. He had also raped me. At that point and I knew I just had to get away from him"

Having reported the domestic violence, Emma was housed by the local council but, in spite of getting away from her ex-partner, she was unable to kick her drug habit - mainly amphetamine and occasionally ecstasy. She did, however, have an extended family network around her new tenancy as her auntie, uncle and cousins all lived within a few streets of her new address.

Emma, who was still only sixteen years old, had not yet developed the necessary life skills to manage a tenancy: "I began letting people into my house and it became a meeting place for all kinds of people. I saw it as company for me."

Her house soon began to be used as a drug den, with people leaving used needles lying around. This reached a head when, she explained, "Someone put some used needles down my drain and when it rained one day they began floating down the street."

This had further consequences both on her tenancy and on her child's custody. When her son's grandparents witnessed what Emma was allowing, they decided not to return the child to her, being concerned for his safety. They soon contacted the police, who denied her the custody of her son.

Having established Emma was not capable of looking after Karl, they expressed the intention of applying for custody of the child; however, only a few weeks later they announced they were splitting up. Nonetheless, her father vowed to continue his fight for custody of his grandchild and asked Emma to move back home to live with him.

Delighted at this upturn, fate took another turn and before they had a chance to go to court, Emma's father collapsed and died of a brain haemorrhage. As a result, she was unable to gain custody without the help of her father and secondly, she was again made homeless.

Although her mother may have been an option, Emma said, "She didn't want me to move in with her and to be honest I wouldn't have wanted to. I basically stayed with whoever I could and continued living like that for a long time."

It was a "horrible" time for Emma: "I was also very depressed about my dad dying and at the memory of finding my Nan dead in her house, knowing she had been dead and neglected for several days when my mum lived in the same street. This made me hate my mum even more."

Her depression, coupled with her homelessness, pushed Emma towards amphetamine once more. This was not helped by Emma becoming involved with the activities of her friends who were committing crimes such as stealing cars and shoplifting. She was eventually caught shoplifting and bailed to attend court. By now Emma had exhausted people's sofas and had begun sleeping on the street. She recalled, "At this time I was sleeping in the graveyard behind Wilkinson's."

After several months of living this way, Emma, who had just turned nineteen, managed to secure a bedsit. This was very short-term, lasting only two months before she was sentenced and sent to prison for the first time.

After serving six weeks, Emma was released. Within four weeks, however, she was again arrested for a similar offence. This time Emma was sentenced to three months in custody plus two further months for not complying with a previous community order.

On her release, Emma was given accommodation in a shared house by a service providing support for vulnerable people, including ex-offenders, where she stayed for around twelve months. Thus, her life seemed to regain some level of stability.

During this time Emma became romantically involved in her second significant relationship and, aged twenty-one, found herself pregnant for a second time. Emma described this as a "destructive relationship". She explained, "We were both on amphetamine and often off our faces."

Seeing where things were going, Emma decided to stop using drugs for the sake of the baby: "My boyfriend, Keith, approached his dad to ask for a bond so we could get a house together. We both managed to get jobs in a working men's club. Keith was a barman and I was a cleaner and we worked hard to make a life for ourselves before the baby was due."

Emma's newfound bliss continued; she and Keith got married, moving into a council house in the process. Unfortunately, once the baby was born, cracks began to appear in their relationship and Emma discovered Keith's infidelity. They separated and eventually divorced after two years.

"I was very unhappy at this point in my life and began drinking," she said. "I even began pinching bottles of beer from the club we worked at, locking myself in the toilet and drinking them to forget how bad life was at home."

Emma was the one to leave the family home and made the decision to leave her daughter with her now ex-husband as she was initially unable to find accommodation suitable for her child. This became a permanent situation when Emma, unable to find long-term accommodation, found herself back on the streets, living from hand to mouth.

Emma had shown maturity by giving custody of her daughter to her husband. She said, "He was a good dad and his parents were also around to give my daughter a proper supportive family network."

Shortly after this, Emma began visiting her old haunts and sleeping out, usually in the local graveyard and sofa-surfing. This became a regular way of living for her for well over twelve months. This cycle only came to an end when Emma, who was then living in a tent she had been given, discovered she was pregnant.

She said, "I had made friends with a few other rough sleepers and had met someone who was as needy as me. I seemed to attract certain types and this relationship was no different, as I experienced an awful amount of physical abuse especially as he took acid and smoked dope all day."

She recalled one such occasion of physical abuse: "I was several months into my pregnancy; he lost it and tried to kill me by wrapping a piece of cord around my neck and trying to strangle me with it."

Emma was given a council property by the local authority shortly after this. Due to her pregnancy and physical injuries, however, she refused to leave the house and as a result soon got into housing benefit arrears. Shortly after this, bailiffs turned up at her house. Emma explained, "This is why for the past ten years-plus I've never been able to get another council property, because of the debt I incurred at that time."

Social services came to Emma's aid, however, and provided her with a bedsit for the short term until they could get her a flat. Nonetheless, she would occasionally allow her ex-partner into the property, as he was still sleeping rough. Unfortunately on one of these occasions she was caught by social services, who swiftly removed her from the property and took away her one-month-old baby. Emma found herself on the street and homeless for a third time.

She found a temporary "home" behind the Salvation Army and was fed by some of the residents who would bring her sandwiches most evenings. At this time she was the victim of a serious sexual assault: "One night I was sleeping out on my own when a bloke I didn't recognise approached and raped me. I knew he was staying in the Salvation Army for a short period but, after considering it, I decided not to report it because I didn't think I'd be believed. It was at this point that I began to use heroin. I needed something else to block out what had happened to me."

Emma reflected, "By this point in my life I'd probably spent more time living on the street than in any form of housing tenancy."

Her criminal activity had also escalated; she began committing street robberies and shoplifting almost daily, mainly when she was drunk. She was eventually caught, charged and given a two-and-a-half-year prison sentence for street robbery.

"While I was in prison I worked out why I always end up in an even worse place," she said. "It's because I can't handle when bad things happen to me and the first thing I do is turn to drink or drugs."

On her release, Emma was offered a house provided by Foundation Housing, an arrangement which again was short-lived as she was imprisoned for a further two-and-a-half years for another street robbery, serving an additional 13 months on top of the sentence given by the judge.

In 2009 Emma was again sentenced, this time for six months, after arranging a drug deal with an undercover. When got out of prison at the end of 2010, Emma vowed to put her life in order and, having maintained a relationship with her brother, moved in with him.

Determined to keep away from her past, Emma moved to Bishop Auckland and, within weeks, moved into a flat with her new partner. Consistent with many of her past experiences, however, violence played a significant role in the relationship and Emma was badly beaten up on more than one occasion. She recalled an occurrence when they had both been drinking heavily: "He deliberately tried to set the flat on fire with me in it when I told him I was leaving him." She admitted, "My choice of partners has more often than not been disastrous".

She continued, "I was moved into a safe house near County Durham by a Housing Association as a temporary measure before eventually moving to West Auckland – where I again ended up meeting someone who was both abusive and controlling."

That relationship ended when Emma, during a heated row originating from one of his assaults, stabbed her partner after asking him to leave her home. She was again sentenced to a two-and-a-half years' imprisonment, but due to the extenuating circumstances, Emma said, "The judge was lenient with me."

Emma served eleven months and, on release, was tagged and moved into a flat in County Durham. She admitted, "I was becoming dangerously accustomed to life in prison. I felt safer there, so I cut my tag off because I wanted to go back.

Emma was in fact recalled and finished off her sentence by serving another four months.

Present Day

Emma was released from prison in early 2014. She admits she still drinks "a little too much on occasions".

She has managed to kick her heroin habit- through self-medication - and has stopped using amphetamine altogether. She has continued to make questionable choices in her relationships, although she describes her present relationship as "promising".

Her relationship with her children remains "fragmented". She sees her daughter regularly and is in contact with both her brother and her mother, with whom she has "mended fences".

Since her last prison release two years ago, Emma has been in stable accommodation for the first time in twenty years.

Author's Note and Acknowledgements

This book is based on real life accounts as told by seven clients whose lives crossed over into homelessness at some point or other.

Most of the material used was taken from interviews conducted for the project "Roofless – Seven True Life Stories of Homelessness".

The idea for the project arose during casual conversations with service users about the lowest points in their lives. Many of those discussions were similar and formed the basis of this book.

If over the course of reading their stories your opinions have been altered in a positive sense, I'm glad to have played a part, however small.

This book involved input from a number of people to whom grateful thanks are due:

To all my colleagues at First Stop Darlington whose tireless efforts supporting our service users is often understated; to all the service users interviewed throughout the course of writing this book, and to Linda Hetherington for proof reading the manuscript, helping "make sense" of the words whilst offering generous advice and encouragement.

Glossary

- **ASBO** – Civil order to protect the public from behaviour likely to cause harassment, alarm or distress.

- **At Risk of Homelessness** – People not homeless but whose current economic status has become precarious, putting them at risk of losing their accommodation.

- **Cannabis** – Also known as Marijuana, a mood altering drug.

- **Claret** – Used to describe blood.

- **Crack Cocaine** – A crystal form of cocaine producing a fast and intense high.

- **CPN** – Community Psychiatric Nurse, a psychiatric nurse based in the community rather than a psychiatric hospital.

- **Ecstasy** – Psychoactive drug used primarily for recreational purposes.

- **Foyer** – Offering affordable accommodation for young people, usually between the ages of sixteen and twenty-five.

- **Harm Reduction** – Refers to programmes and practices aimed at reducing risks and negative effects associated with substance misuse and addictive behaviours.

- **Heroin** – Used as a recreational drug known for its highly addictive and euphoric effect.

- **Inadequate Housing** – Housing requiring major repairs and/or displaying significant damage.

- **LSD (Acid)** – Psychedelic drug also known for its psychological effects.
- **NFA** – Being of no fixed abode or address.

- **PNC** – A computer system used by the police (Police National Computer).

- **Refuge** – A place or situation providing safety or shelter.

- **Rattling** – Desperate for the next fix or withdrawing from drugs.

- **Rough Sleeping** – People sleeping or bedded down in the open air, in places such as streets or doorways, not designed for habitation.

- **Sofa-Surfing** – The practice of staying temporarily with various friends and relatives while attempting to find permanent accommodation.

- **Squat** – The unlawfully occupancy of an uninhabited building.

- **Substance Use** – Refers to all types of drug and alcohol.

- **Score** – Purchase drugs.

- **Tracks** – Marks left by a needle on the skin of someone using illegal drugs.